CHARLIE BROWN'S
'CYCLOPEDIA

Super Questions and Answers and Amazing Facts

Featuring
Your Body

Volume 1

Based on the Charles M. Schulz Characters

Funk & Wagnalls, Inc.

ISBN: 0-394-84550-1

3 4 5 6 7 8 9 0

A large part of the material in this volume was previously published in *Charlie Brown's Super Book of Questions and Answers.*

Introduction

Welcome to volume 1 of *Charlie Brown's 'Cyclopedia!* Have you ever wondered how many bones there are in your body, or why you're ticklish, or what makes your foot "go to sleep"? Charlie Brown and the rest of the *Peanuts* gang are here to help you find the answers to these questions and many more about your body. Have fun!

You and How You Grow

What are you made of?

Yes, you are made of cells. Every part of you—your bones, your muscles, your skin, your blood, your nerves, your teeth, your hair—is made of cells. These cells are so tiny that you can see them only under a microscope. Your whole body is made up of trillions and trillions of them.

What do cells look like?

This is a picture of one tiny cell as it looks under a microscope.

Not all cells look exactly like this one. Different parts of your body are made up of different kinds of cells.

Each kind of cell does a special job that no other kind of cell can do. For example, muscle cells can tighten and relax to make your body move. One kind of blood cell can kill harmful germs. Nerve cells can send messages to your brain and other parts of your body.

Muscle cells

Blood cells

Skin cells

Nerve cells

Bone cells

What makes you grow?

You grow because the cells of your body keep dividing into new cells. When you eat, your cells take in food and grow bigger. Then each cell divides and becomes two cells. Then each of the two cells divides, making four cells, and so on. As the number of cells in your body becomes greater, you grow bigger and bigger.

Lucy's trick isn't going to work. No matter how often she pushes on Linus's head, she won't be able to stop him from growing.

When did you start growing?

You started growing from just two cells about nine months before you were born. One cell, a sperm cell, came from your father. Another cell, an egg cell, came from your mother. The two cells joined together inside your mother's body. They formed a special new cell called a fertilized egg. This cell was the start of a whole human being—you.

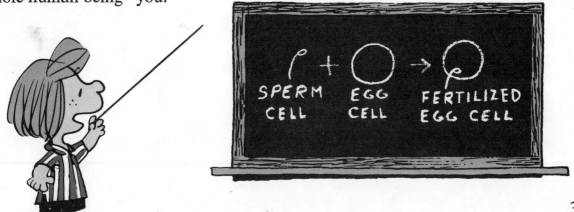

3

How does a fertilized egg cell become a whole person?

A fertilized egg starts out the size of the head of a pin. It settles inside a special place in the mother's body called the uterus (YOU-ter-us). Then the fertilized egg grows and divides in half. It becomes two cells that are just alike. Then these cells grow and divide. The new cells divide again and again. More and more cells keep developing. But after a while, not all of them look alike. Some are muscle cells, some are bone cells, some are nerve cells, some are blood cells. All the different kinds of cells that make up a human body are there.

About a week after the fertilized egg began to divide, the new cells start to grow into special body parts—brain, heart, and lungs, for example. After about two months, the developing baby has eyes, ears, a nose, and a mouth. It has tiny legs and arms, too. It has a complete heart that beats and sends blood through its body. But it is still less than an inch long. For seven more months, the baby keeps developing in its mother's body. It grows bigger and heavier. It looks more and more like a person. At last—about nine months after the fertilized egg began to divide—the baby is born.

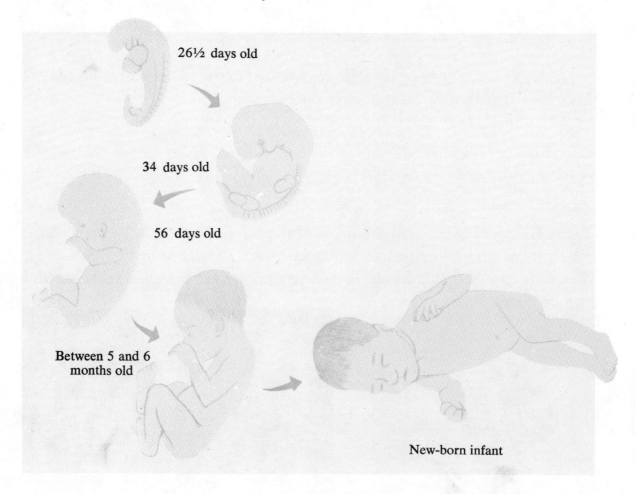

26½ days old

34 days old

56 days old

Between 5 and 6 months old

New-born infant

4

How big is a newborn baby?

When a baby is born, it is usually about 20 inches long, and it probably weighs between six and nine pounds.

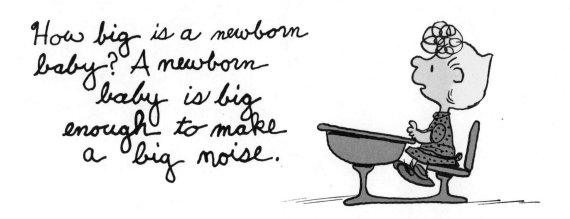

How big is a newborn baby? A newborn baby is big enough to make a big noise.

How do twins start growing?

When two sperm cells join with two egg cells at the same time, twins begin to grow. These twins are known as fraternal twins. The two children don't have to look at all alike.

Twins that look alike are called identical twins. These start growing from just one fertilized egg cell. The cell begins to divide and grow. After a few days of growth, the group of cells separates into two parts. The two parts are exactly alike. Each part grows into a whole person.

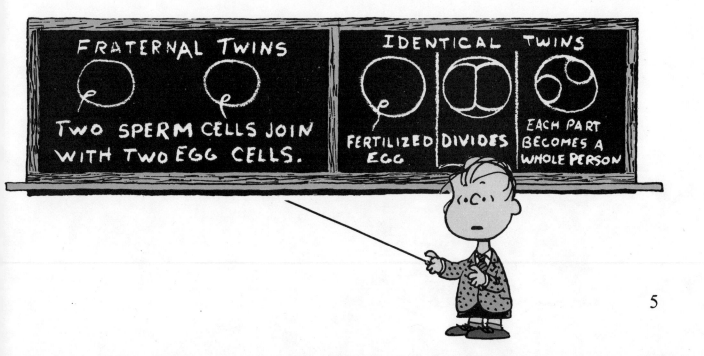

FRATERNAL TWINS

TWO SPERM CELLS JOIN WITH TWO EGG CELLS.

IDENTICAL TWINS

FERTILIZED EGG | DIVIDES | EACH PART BECOMES A WHOLE PERSON

Why do you have a "belly button"?

Before you were born, you and your mother were connected in her uterus by a tube called an umbilical cord. The cord was attached to you on the spot where your "belly button" is now. Everything you needed to live and grow—including food and oxygen—came to you from your mother through this cord.

After you were born, you no longer needed the umbilical cord because you could eat, drink, and breathe for yourself. So the doctor carefully tied the cord and cut it off as close to your belly as possible. But a tiny piece of the cord was left. This piece began to dry up, and it fell off about a week after you were born. A little dent was left in your belly. The dent is called your navel, or belly button.

When will you stop growing?

If you are a girl, you will stop growing when you are about 18 years old. If you are a boy, you may keep growing taller for a few more years. After you reach your full height, you may get fatter, but you won't get any taller.

Your Skeleton

FOR "SHOW AND TELL" TODAY, I WANT TO TALK TO YOU ABOUT YOUR SKELETON. IT HAS 206 BONES AND 32 TEETH.

Why do you need a skeleton?

Your skeleton is the framework of your body. It holds you up and gives your body its shape. Because bones are hard and strong, your skeleton also protects important parts of you, such as your heart, lungs, and brain.

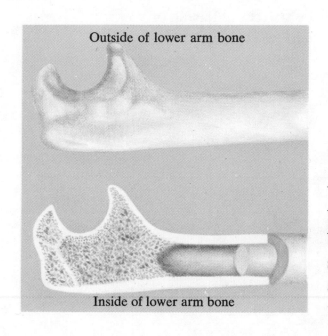

Outside of lower arm bone

Inside of lower arm bone

What do bones look like?

Your bones look somewhat like the beef bone Snoopy has in his mouth, but they are different shapes and sizes. On the outside, they are white and hard and strong. On the inside, they are soft and spongy.

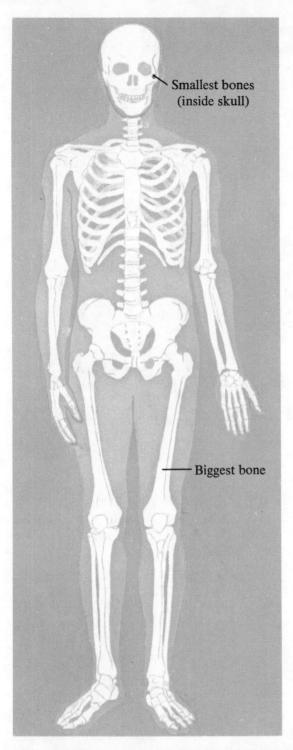

Smallest bones (inside skull)

Biggest bone

What are the smallest bones in your body?

Three tiny bones in your ear, deep inside your head, are the smallest. The three together are about the size of your thumbnail. These bones look like their names—the hammer, the anvil, and the stirrup.

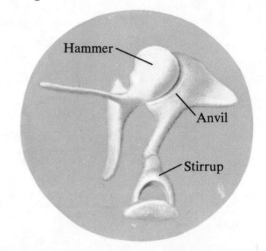

Hammer

Anvil

Stirrup

What are your biggest bones?

Your thigh bones, or femurs (FEE-mers), are the biggest. If you grow up to be six feet tall, each of your thigh bones will be almost 20 inches long.

Nearly half the bones in your body are in your hands and feet!

FOR "SHOW AND TELL" TODAY I HAVE BROUGHT YOU A LOCAL HERO!

THIS LITTLE FELLOW HERE BROKE HIS FIFTH METATARSAL WHILE RESCUING THREE AIRLINE STEWARDESSES ON RUNAWAY HORSES!

LISTEN CAREFULLY, FOR THIS IS THE WAY IT ALL HAPPENED...

INCIDENTALLY, MA'AM, ARE WE GRADED ON TRUTH AND ACCURACY?

Can your bones bend?

No. Your bones cannot bend. You bend your arms, your legs, and other parts of your body at the places where two bones join together. These places are called joints. You bend only at your joints.

Why do you need a cast when you have a broken arm or leg?

When you say you have a broken arm, you really mean that you have a broken or fractured (cracked) bone in your arm. In order for the broken parts to heal, they must be held in place. A cast does this job.

When a doctor puts a cast on a broken arm, he first places the broken parts together the way he wants them to heal. Then he puts layers of gauze bandage and wet plaster around the arm. The plaster hardens with the gauze and forms a firm cast. That keeps the broken ends of the bone from moving around, so that they can grow together again.

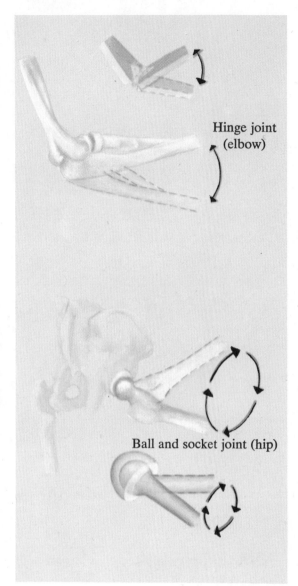

Hinge joint (elbow)

Ball and socket joint (hip)

What is a "funny bone"?

A "funny bone" is not a bone at all. It's a nerve at the back of your elbow close to the bone. "Funny bone" is just an expression. When you hit your funny bone, you get a painful tingling feeling in your arm. As Charlie Brown can tell you, it's not very funny!

Why do your baby teeth fall out?

Your baby teeth fall out to make room for larger and stronger teeth. Everyone grows two sets of teeth. When you were about six months old, your first set of teeth started to come through your gums. These were your baby teeth. You had 20 of them, and they were very small.

These baby teeth did not grow larger after they came through your gums. But the rest of your body kept growing. So after a few years, your baby teeth became too small for your jaw. But in the meantime, a set of larger and stronger teeth were growing inside your gums. One by one, these larger teeth have been pushing through your gums, and your baby teeth have been falling out to make room for the new ones. The second set of teeth are called permanent teeth.

Do wisdom teeth make you smarter?

No. Wisdom teeth are simply the last four teeth that come into your mouth. You may not get them until you are a teen-ager or even an adult. Because they appear at so late an age, people call them them wisdom teeth. By the time you get these teeth, you should have grown pretty wise.

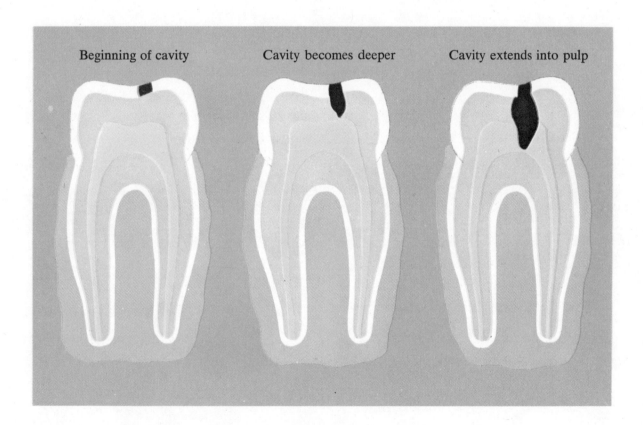

Beginning of cavity — Cavity becomes deeper — Cavity extends into pulp

How do you get a cavity in your tooth?

After you eat, tiny bits of food are left between your teeth. If you don't brush away these food bits, germs grow on them and start to eat away at the hard outside part of your teeth. The hole that the germs make is called a cavity.

How can you prevent cavities?

You can prevent cavities by brushing away the food left in your mouth after you eat. Then the germs will have nothing to grow on. Brushing after every meal works best. You should also use dental floss every night to get out all the bits stuck between your teeth.

You can also help prevent cavities by not eating foods with a lot of sugar in them. Cavity-making germs grow best in sugar.

You should also visit your dentist twice a year. The dentist will check to see if you have any cavities. If you do, he will clean them out to get rid of the germs. Then he will fill the holes with silver or porcelain (POUR-suh-lin). The cavities will not grow any deeper and give you a toothache.

What causes a toothache?

When a cavity gets very deep, you will have a toothache. Inside each tooth is a soft, sensitive area with nerves in it. When a cavity reaches that area — OUCH! — it hurts!

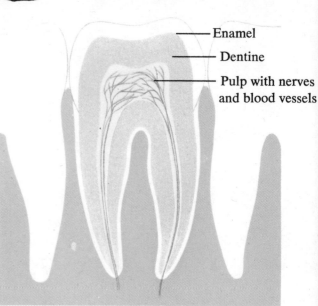

— Enamel

— Dentine

— Pulp with nerves and blood vessels

Your Muscles

Why do you need muscles?

You need muscles in order to move. A muscle is a bundle of cells that can tighten up and get shorter. Then it can relax again and go back to its normal size. When a muscle tightens up, a part of you moves.

For example, two muscles are at work when you bend your arm at the elbow. These muscles are called the biceps (BY-seps) and triceps (TRY-seps). Each of them is attached to two bones—one at your shoulder and one below your elbow. When you want to bend your arm, your brain sends a message to your biceps to tighten up. When the biceps tightens, it gets shorter, and it pulls up the lower part of your arm. When you want to straighten your arm out again, your brain sends a message to the triceps to tighten up. This muscle gets shorter and pulls your arm back down. At the same time, your biceps relaxes.

You can easily feel your biceps at work. Put your hand on your arm above the elbow. Now bend your arm. You will feel your biceps tightening up. Straighten your arm back down again. You will feel the muscle relax and go back to its normal size.

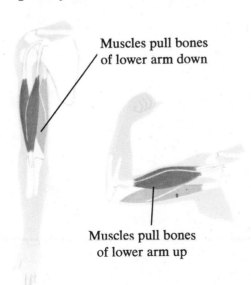

Muscles pull bones of lower arm down

Muscles pull bones of lower arm up

Why do some people have bigger muscles than other people?

The size of your muscles depends on how much you use them. When you do easy things such as sitting, standing, walking, or eating, you use only a small part of each muscle. But when you run, dance, play ball, or swim, you make your muscles work very hard. If you make a muscle work hard very often, it becomes much bigger and stronger. That's why ice skaters have large leg muscles and boxers have large arm muscles.

What is a "charley horse"?

A "charley horse" is not a horse at all. It is a kind of muscle cramp. If you exercise too much and make a muscle work harder than it ever has before, you may get a charley horse. If you do, the muscle will begin to tighten up when you don't want it to, and it will hurt. Resting the muscle and keeping it warm will help it to relax again.

14

Why do you shiver on a cold day?

Shivering helps to make you feel warmer. When you shiver, some of your muscles tighten and relax very quickly, over and over again. The muscles work hard —without your thinking about them working or even wanting them to. When your muscles work hard, you warm up.

If you play ball or run a lot on a cold day, you won't shiver. By exercising, you are already making your muscles work very hard. The exercise warms you up.

15

Your Skin and Hair

WOODSTOCK HAS SKIN *AND* FEATHERS TO PROTECT HIM.

Why do you need skin?

How strange you would look walking around with your insides showing! Your skin covers your body, but it does more than that. It keeps many germs out of your body, and so stops them from harming you. It also protects the large amount of water that is in your body. If you did not have skin, your body would dry out and shrivel up like a raisin.

What are wrinkles?

Wrinkles are little folds in a person's skin. When you grow much older, you will probably get some wrinkles on your face. Attached to the skin on your face are more than 25 muscles. If these muscles don't get enough exercise over the years, they will become weak. Then they won't be able to hold your skin tightly to your face any more. Your skin will sag, and little wrinkles will appear.

Wrinkles can also be caused by staying in the sun too much. Too much sun dries out the oils in your skin. Without these oils, skin gets dry and wrinkly.

16

Why do you get "goose pimples"?

"Goose pimples" are tiny bumps that sometimes come out on your skin when you are cold or frightened. If you look closely at the bumps, you will see a hair in the middle of each one. Attached to each hair, inside your skin, is a tiny muscle. When you get scared or chilled, each of these muscles tightens up and gets short. The muscles pull the hairs and make them stand straight up. The skin around each hair is pulled up, too. The result is little bumps. We call these bumps goose pimples because they look just like the bumps on the skin of a plucked goose!

THIS GOOSE IS GIVING ME GOOSE PIMPLES.

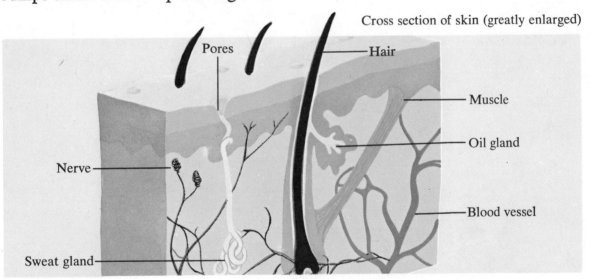

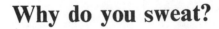
Cross section of skin (greatly enlarged)

Pores — Hair — Muscle — Oil gland — Blood vessel — Nerve — Sweat gland

Why do you sweat?

BOY, IT'S HOT TODAY!

You sweat to cool off. Your body is always making heat. When you exercise, your muscles make extra heat. On a hot summer day, the sun heats up your body, too. If your body did not get rid of some of the extra heat, your temperature would get too high. A very high temperature could kill you. So your body lets heat escape through your skin by sweating.

When you sweat, moisture comes out of your skin. The moisture has heat in it. It evaporates—disappears into the air—carrying the heat with it. Then you feel cooler.

Your skin weighs twice as much as your brain!

Why do people have different-colored skin?

The color of your skin depends on how much pigment, or coloring matter, you have in it. All people have some brown and some yellow pigments in their skins. But everybody has a different amount of each pigment. The amount you have depends on the amount your parents have. Because people have such different amounts of the two pigments, many shades of skin color exist in the world. "Black" people have a lot of brown pigment in their skin and not much yellow. "White" people have a small amount of each pigment in their skin. Oriental people have a lot of yellow and a small amount of brown pigment.

THINK OF IT THIS WAY PATTY · FRECKLES ARE A SIGN OF BEAUTY IN SOME CULTURES!

Why do some people have freckles?

Freckles are caused by the brown skin pigment called melanin (MEL-uh-nin). All of us have some melanin in our skins. If you have a lot of it, and it is bunched up in spots, you will have freckles, just as Peppermint Patty does.

When sunlight hits your skin, the skin makes more melanin than usual. So, although you may not have freckles most of the time, you may get them in the sun.

What is an albino?

An albino (al-BY-no) is a person whose skin does not have any coloring matter in it. Albinos also have no pigment in their hair and eyes, as other people do. Albinos have very pale white skin, very light blonde hair, and pink eyes. An albino's eyes are pink because they have no coloring matter to cover up the tiny red blood vessels that are in everyone's eyes. A person can have parents of any color and still be an albino.

What are fingerprints?

Look at the tips of your fingers. Do you see the swirls and loops made by the ridges of the skin? They form the designs that make fingerprints whenever your fingers touch something. Your fingerprints are different from everybody else's in the world. They get bigger as you grow. But otherwise they stay exactly the same all through your life.

!

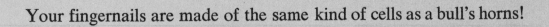

Your fingernails are made of the same kind of cells as a bull's horns!

What is a wart?

A wart is a small hard bump that sometimes comes out on your skin. Many people think that you can get a wart by touching a toad. But you can't. A wart is caused by very tiny germs called viruses that get into your skin. If you pick on a wart and it opens, the viruses can spread to any part of your body that the wart touches. They can even spread to other people. Then more warts can grow —on you or on someone else.

Can you get rid of warts in a graveyard at midnight?

No. Many strange stories have grown up about ways to get rid of warts, but none of them are true. One story is that you can get rid of a wart by taking a dead cat to a graveyard at midnight—the way Tom Sawyer did in *The Adventures of Tom Sawyer*. This method is adventurous, but it doesn't work. There are only two safe ways to get rid of a wart. You can wait for it to go away by itself. It usually will, but only after a long time. Or, if you don't want to wait, you can have a doctor remove the wart.

What is blushing?

The way you feel can affect your body. Sometimes, when you feel embarrassed or ashamed, you blush. Your face and neck look red and feel very warm. Tiny blood vessels in your skin are getting larger and bringing more blood to the top part of your skin. The blood shows through your skin and makes it look red. The blood brings heat with it, so your face and neck also feel warm.

Why do some people have curly hair and others straight hair?

Hair is naturally curly or naturally straight because of the way it grows. Look at one of your hairs. It seems very skinny, doesn't it? But it does have some thickness. If the hair is a curly one, it did not grow evenly all the way through. Some parts of it grew faster than others. This caused the hair to twist around, or curl. If your hair is a straight one, it grew evenly all the way through. And so it did not curl.

Whether you have curly hair or straight hair depends on the kind of hair your parents and your grandparents have.

How fast does the hair on your head grow?

In a month, your hair grows about three-quarters of an inch! Even when you stop growing taller, your hair will still keep growing. It grows faster in the summer than in the winter. It grows faster during the day than at night.

How long can hair grow?

Very long! A man in India had hair that grew to be 26 feet long! But most people's hair never gets longer than 3 or 4 feet.

Your Brain and Nervous System

What does your brain do?

Your brain controls everything you think about and just about everything you do. Your brain controls breathing, seeing, hearing, and feeling hungry. It controls laughing, reading a book, playing the piano, talking, walking, and crying. Your brain lets you learn new things. Your brain also lets you remember things that happened three days ago or three years ago.

Feeling hungry

Reading

Playing piano

How can your brain control all these things?

Your brain is the headquarters of a giant message system called your nervous system. Your brain gets messages from every part of your body by way of special long cells called nerves. Your brain then sends its own messages back through the nerves to tell the different parts of your body what to do.

For example, suppose a fly walks across your neck and tickles it. Nerves from your neck send a "tickle message" to your brain. Your brain decides what should be done next. If it decides the tickle should be scratched, your brain sends a message to your arm to lift. It sends a message to your hand to scratch. So you lift your arm and scratch your neck.

Laughing

Crying

Remembering

23

What is your spinal cord?

Your spinal cord is a long cord made of nerve cells. It runs from your brain all the way down your back inside the bones of your spine. Most nerve messages pass through your spinal cord on their way to and from your brain.

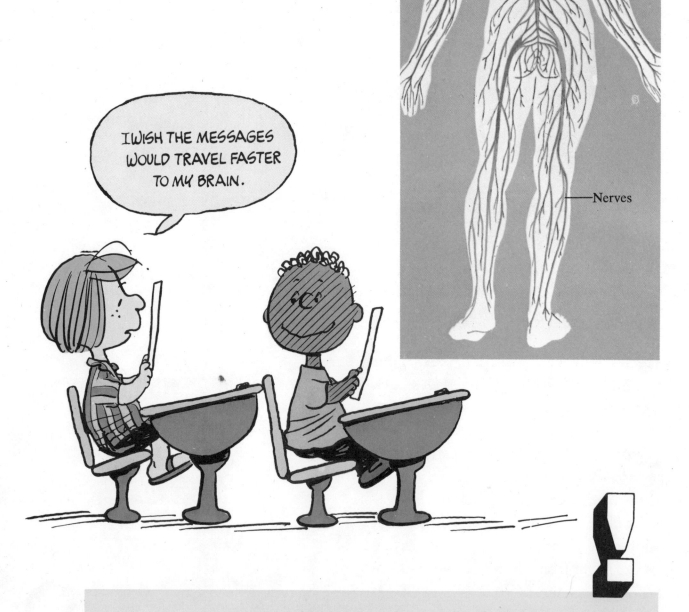

Some messages travel along your nerves at a speed of 200 miles an hour!

Why do you drop a hot potato?

You drop a hot potato before you even feel the pain that comes from burning your hand. As soon as you touch the potato, nerves quickly send a message: "Too hot!" This special danger message goes straight to your spinal cord. Right away, nerves in your spinal cord answer the message. They don't wait for the

message to reach your brain. These nerves make you spread out your fingers so you will drop the potato. You don't even have to think about opening your hand. Then the message goes from your spinal cord to your brain. Your brain makes you realize that the potato was too hot to touch—that touching it caused you pain. You'll be more careful next time. Any danger message is answered by your spinal cord before it goes to your brain, so that you can act very quickly.

Do smarter people have bigger brains?

No. The size of your brain does not affect how smart you are. The brains of most grownups are about the same size and weight, although there are slight differences. It is very possible for a genius to have a smaller brain than a stupid person.

Your brain weighs more than a horse's brain, but less than an elephant's!

Which is smarter—a computer or the human brain?

The human brain is smarter, but a computer works faster. Computers can do only what people tell them—or "program" them—to do. They cannot think of anything new, while the human brain is always coming up with new ideas. However, a computer is very fast. It can, for example, solve in a few minutes a mathematical problem that might take a person many, many years to figure out.

What happens when you sleep?

When you sleep most of your brain and many of your nerves "turn off." Very few messages can then be sent to or from your brain. For example, when you are asleep you can't hear the TV in the next room. And if someone turns on a light in your room, you don't notice it. But while you sleep, many things continue to go on in your body. Your heart beats, you breathe, and you dream. Your body also replaces worn-out cells.

No one knows for sure why you sleep. Some scientists think your body needs a chance to rest and repair itself. Others disagree. Whatever the reason, you usually feel stronger and healthier after a good night's sleep.

During your lifetime, your brain may store
up to 100 million bits of information!

Why are some people left-handed?

Although most people are right-handed, some are left-handed, and a few can use one hand as well as the other. We say these people are ambidextrous (am-bih-DECK-struss). Not all scientists agree on what causes these differences. But many think this is the answer:

Each side of your brain controls the muscles on the opposite side of your body. In most people the left side of the brain is more powerful (dominant) than the right side. These people have better control over the muscles on their right side. If the left side of your brain is dominant, you are right-handed. If the right side of your brain is dominant, you are left-handed. If both sides of your brain are about equal, you may be ambidextrous.

Not very long ago, parents and teachers used to try and change left-handed children into right-handed children. Today scientists know that it is best for left-handed children to stay the way they are. Forcing them to use their right hand confuses the two sides of the brain.

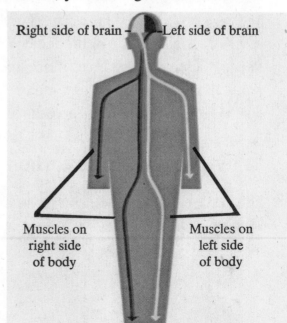

Right side of brain — Left side of brain

Muscles on right side of body

Muscles on left side of body

Your Senses

Why are you ticklish?

When you are lightly touched, special nerve cells inside your skin pick up the feeling. They send a message to your brain. Your brain can interpret or make sense of the message in several different ways. If your brain interprets the message as an unpleasant feeling, we say you are ticklish. If your brain interprets the message as a pleasant light touch, you are not ticklish. The touch doesn't bother you.

Why must you feel pain?

Have you ever wished that you couldn't feel pain? Well, you are lucky that you *can* feel it. Pain protects you and warns you that something is wrong.

For example, when you have an earache, nerve cells in the ear send a message of pain to your brain. Then your brain knows that something is wrong inside your ear. Your brain decides what you should do about the problem—go to the doctor, for instance. If you didn't feel the pain in your ear, you would not know that something was wrong with it. The trouble could get worse and worse, and your ear might end up badly damaged.

Why doesn't it hurt when your hair and nails are cut?

Hair and nails both have no nerves in them. Without nerve cells to send a message of pain to your spinal cord and brain, you can cut your hair and nails and never feel a thing.

How do you taste different flavors?

You taste with your tongue, your nose, and your brain. Stick out your tongue and look in the mirror. You will see little bumps on your tongue. Inside each of those bumps are about a dozen tiny taste buds. Nerves carry "taste messages" from these taste buds to your brain.

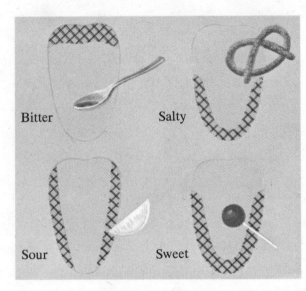

Location of taste buds

You have four kinds of taste buds on your tongue. The different kinds are in different places. In the back of your tongue you taste bitter foods. You taste sour things on the sides. You taste sweet and salty foods both on the sides of your tongue and at the tip.

But that is only the beginning of tasting. In order to taste the special flavors of foods, you need your nose. The smell of foods plays a big part in how they taste. That is why foods have very little flavor when you have a cold and your nose is all stuffed up.

Why do you sniff to smell a flower?

Everything that has a smell gives off a small amount of gas. You smell something when the gas touches special nerve cells high up in your nose. They send a "smell message" to your brain. Many flowers have a very weak smell. You must sniff to bring the flower's gas up to your smelling nerve cells.

How do you hear?

When sounds are made, they set up movements in the air. These movements are called sound waves. The outside part of the ear collects the sound waves. They move through the inside parts of your ear to nerve cells. The nerves pass the "message" of the sound waves to your brain—and then you hear!

What is your eardrum?

Your eardrum is a tough sheet of cells inside your ear. The sheet is stretched tight—like the skin across the top of a drum. When sound waves enter your ear, they hit the eardrum. The eardrum begins to move quickly—or vibrate—the way a drum does when it is hit. This vibration causes three tiny bones in your ear to vibrate, too. They in turn cause vibrations in a liquid that fills the deepest part of your ear. The moving liquid presses on your hearing nerve cells, which pass the sound message on to your brain.

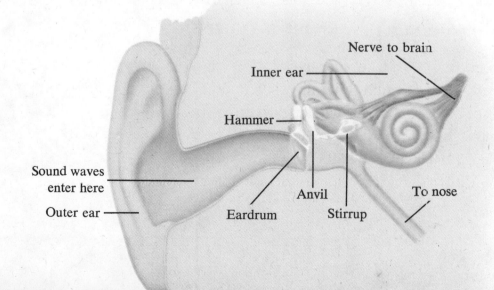

Is it true that your eye is like a camera?

Yes, it's true. A camera has a diaphragm (DIE-uh-fram) that gets bigger or smaller to let in the right amount of light. Your eye has an iris that does the same thing. A camera has a lens that focuses the light into a clear picture. Your eye also has a lens to focus the light. In a camera, the light forms a picture on film. In your eye, the picture is formed on the retina (RET-uh-nuh), all the way in the back of your eye. The picture is upside down on both the film and the retina.

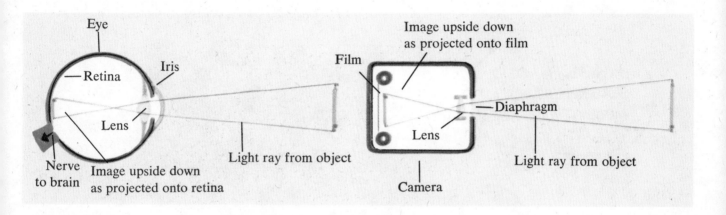

Eye

Retina

Iris

Lens

Nerve to brain

Image upside down as projected onto retina

Light ray from object

Image upside down as projected onto film

Film

Diaphragm

Lens

Camera

Light ray from object

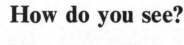

How do you see?
You see with your eyes.
That is how you see.
The end.

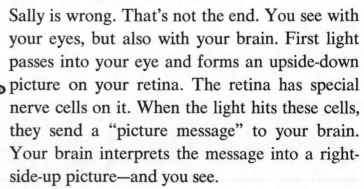

How do you see?

Sally is wrong. That's not the end. You see with your eyes, but also with your brain. First light passes into your eye and forms an upside-down picture on your retina. The retina has special nerve cells on it. When the light hits these cells, they send a "picture message" to your brain. Your brain interprets the message into a right-side-up picture—and you see.

Why do some people have to wear eyeglasses?

Some people need glasses because they can't see clearly without them. Three of the most common eye problems are being nearsighted, being farsighted, and having an astigmatism (uh-STIG-muh-tiz-um).

If you are nearsighted, you can see things clearly only if they are very near. If you are farsighted, you can see things clearly only if they are far away. If you have an astigmatism, things look blurry whether they are near or far. All three problems can be corrected with eyeglasses. Glasses help to focus the light properly so that you can see clearly all the time.

HONESTLY MARCIE. GLASSES GIVE YOU A MORE INTELLECTUAL LOOK.

TRUE. TRUE.

Why do so many grandparents wear eyeglasses?

When people get older, their eyes usually cannot focus as well as they used to. Things look fuzzy. So these people wear eyeglasses to correct the problem.

People have been wearing eyeglasses
for more than 700 years!

What does it mean to be color-blind?

A color-blind person cannot tell all colors apart. Most color-blind people can see shades of yellow and blue pretty well, but red and green look alike to them. A few color-blind people cannot see any colors. They see everything in black, white, and shades of grey. More boys are color-blind than girls.

What is ESP?

ESP stands for "extrasensory perception." These two words mean "awareness outside the senses." Usually, we use our five senses to understand the world around us. We see, hear, taste, smell, and feel. ESP means getting certain information about the world without using any of the five senses. Some examples of ESP are reading someone's mind, knowing the future, and dreaming about something as it happens many miles away. Some people seem able to do these things. Scientists have been doing experiments for many years to find out if ESP really exists. But so far no one has proved that it does.

The Food You Eat

Why do you eat?

Eating is fun, especially when you are hungry and you like the food. But you really eat to feed your cells, so that your body can grow healthy and strong. You eat so that you can have the energy to play and work.

Why do you get thirsty?

Your body has a lot of water in it—salt water. You must have certain amounts of both salt and water in your body at all times. When you eat a lot of extra salt, your body has too much salt in it for the amount of water. The same thing is true when you lose a lot of water. The thirsty feeling is a signal to drink more water and get the salt and water levels back to normal.

34

What happens to the food you eat?

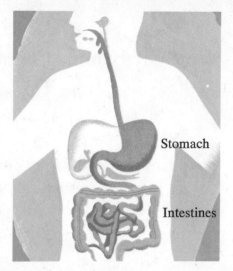

Stomach

Intestines

You digest (die-GEST) it. That means that your body breaks the food down into pieces small enough to enter your tiny cells.

You start breaking down the food in your mouth. Your teeth chew it into very small pieces. When you swallow the food, it moves down a tube to your stomach. From your stomach it passes through a long, thin coiled tube called the small intestine. All along the way it is broken down more and more by juices —digestive juices—that are made in your body. Finally, in your small intestine, most of the food becomes a liquid. The liquid goes into your blood and travels around your body to feed all your cells. The parts of the food that you can't use soon go into a fat coiled tube called the large intestine. Then they leave your body as waste.

Why does your mouth water when you smell food?

Your mouth waters because the smell of food starts your digestion going. The "water" that comes into your mouth is not really water at all. It's a digestive juice called saliva (suh-LIE-vuh). There is always some saliva in your mouth. When you eat, a lot more of it flows in to start digesting your food.

But you don't have to put food into your mouth to start the saliva flowing. Just the smell of good food is enough. In fact, you can make your mouth water without even seeing or smelling food. Wait until you're very hungry and then think of your favorite food. Bet your mouth waters!

35

Why does your stomach rumble when you're hungry?

When you eat, food goes into your stomach. There, a digestive juice called gastric juice helps to break down the food. At the same time, muscles in your stomach start working. They cause the sides of your stomach to move. The movement churns the food and rolls it around to help break it down faster.

Because you usually have your meals at the same time each day, your stomach gets right to work at those times—even when you haven't eaten. If there is nothing in your stomach, all that churning can sometimes get noisy.

Why do you burp?

You burp to get rid of gas in your stomach. When you eat fast, you swallow a lot of air. Air is a gas. Too much air in your stomach makes you feel uncomfortable. Your body gets rid of it by forcing the air back out through your mouth. If you drink something with a lot of fizz in it, you may also have to burp. The burp lets the fizzy gas out of your stomach.

What kind of food should you eat?

If you want to keep your body healthy, you must feed it vitamins, minerals, proteins, fats, sugars and starches every day. You can get all of these by eating a variety of fruits, and vegetables; meat, fish, poultry, or eggs; milk or cheese; and cereal or bread.

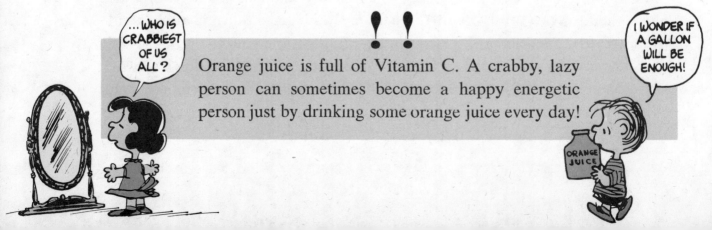

Orange juice is full of Vitamin C. A crabby, lazy person can sometimes become a happy energetic person just by drinking some orange juice every day!

Breathing In, Breathing Out

Why do you breathe?

You breathe to stay alive. When you take a breath, you take air into your body. In the air is a gas called oxygen that your body must have. Oxygen changes the food you have eaten into energy. Your body uses the energy to keep you warm, make new cells, move your muscles, and send messages along your nerves. You need the energy to do anything and everything.

What happens when you breathe?

When you breathe in, air goes through breathing passages in your nose. From your nose the air goes into a tube called your windpipe and then down into your lungs. There, oxygen is taken from the air. The oxygen then passes into your bloodstream. Your blood carries the oxygen around your body to all your cells.

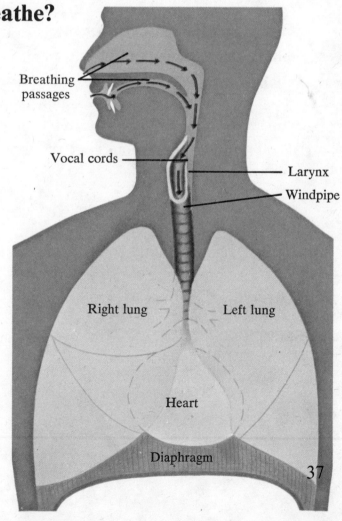

At the same time, your blood picks up a waste gas called carbon dioxide from all your cells. Your blood carries the carbon dioxide to your lungs. When you breathe out, you get rid of this carbon dioxide along with the leftover air. Muscles between your ribs and under your lungs tighten and relax to pump these gases in and out.

37

How do you talk?

Put your fingers on your throat and say, "Yes." Do you get a buzzing feeling on your fingers? The buzzing comes from the "voice box"—or larynx—inside your throat.

Inside your larynx are two vocal chords. When you speak, air comes from your lungs and passes between the vocal cords. It makes them vibrate—move back and forth very quickly. The buzz you feel when you touch your throat is your vocal cords vibrating. The vibration causes a sound. Your lips and tongue help to make the sound into the word "yes."

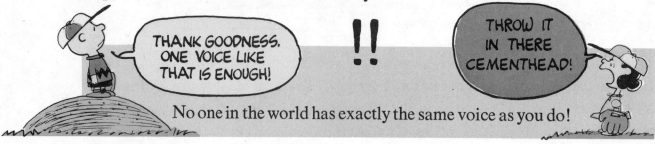

THANK GOODNESS. ONE VOICE LIKE THAT IS ENOUGH!

!!

THROW IT IN THERE CEMENTHEAD!

No one in the world has exactly the same voice as you do!

What is an Adam's apple?

An Adam's apple is a hard protective covering around the larynx. It looks like a lump bulging out of a person's neck. The Adam's apple is made of cartilage cells—special bonelike cells that also make up your ears and the tip of your nose. Everyone has an Adam's apple. But some Adam's apples are easier to see than others. Run your hand up and down the front of your neck. You should feel a small lump near the top, under your chin. That's your Adam's apple.

How did the Adam's apple get its name?

WOULD YOU CARE FOR AN APPLE CHARLIE BROWN?

A long time ago, people didn't know what the lump on their neck really was. They didn't know about cartilage cells or about the larynx either. So they made up a story to explain what they didn't understand. They said that when Adam, in the Bible, ate the forbidden apple in the Garden of Eden, a piece of apple got stuck in his throat. So all people after him had a lump in their throat—the Adam's apple.

GOOD GRIEF, LINUS! YOU ARE ALLERGIC TO GOLDENROD!

KACHOO!

The longest record of sneezing without stopping is 155 days!

Why do you sneeze?

You sneeze to get rid of something that is bothering one of your breathing passages. You may have dust up your nose, or you may have pollen—the powder that comes from flowers. A message goes to your spinal cord saying, "Get rid of it!" Your spinal cord then sends a message to your breathing muscles. They tighten and relax to make you suddenly breathe in and out with a lot of force—kachoo! And out goes the dust or the pollen from your nose.

When you have a cold, you sneeze because cold germs are irritating your breathing passages—making them sore. Sneezing gets rid of some germs, but it can't stop the soreness. So you keep on sneezing as long as your breathing passages are irritated.

Why can't you breathe underwater?

Your body needs to breathe oxygen. There is oxygen in water, but your lungs are not built to separate it from the water. They can take oxygen only from air. If you tried to breathe underwater, water would fill up your lungs, and you would drown.

Why can't you hold your breath for more than a few minutes?

Your body has a built-in protection against holding your breath a long time. When you stop breathing, you begin to store up carbon dioxide. If there is too much of this gas in your blood, a message goes to the part of your brain that controls breathing. Your brain sends back a message to your breathing muscles to start working. Soon you are forced to breathe again, no matter how hard you try to hold your breath.

Your Heart and Blood

Does your heart look like a valentine heart?

No. Your heart is not as pretty as a valentine heart, but it's much more valuable. It keeps you alive by pumping blood through your body.

Make a fist with your hand. That's about the size of your heart. That's about the shape of your heart, too.

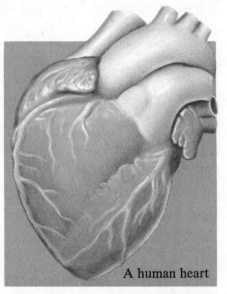

A human heart

What does your doctor hear through a stethoscope?

Lubb-dup, lubb-dup, lubb-dup. That's the steady rhythm your doctor hears through a stethoscope when listening to your heart. The heart is a muscle that is constantly tightening and relaxing as it pumps blood. We call this constant movement your heartbeat. The lubb-dups are the sound of the strong valves of your heart opening and closing as your heart beats. These valves act like one-way doors, letting the blood in or out of the heart. The doctor can tell by the sound of the lubb-dups if your heart is working properly.

WOODSTOCK, YOUR HEART RHYTHM TELLS ME YOU NEED A LITTLE REST. I'M GROUNDING YOU FOR A MONTH!

BLEAH!

How fast does your heart beat?

Normally, your heart beats about 70 to 80 times a minute. When you are exercising, your heartbeat is faster. When you are sleeping, your heartbeat is slower.

Your heart beats more than 36 million times a year!

NO WONDER I FEEL TIRED!

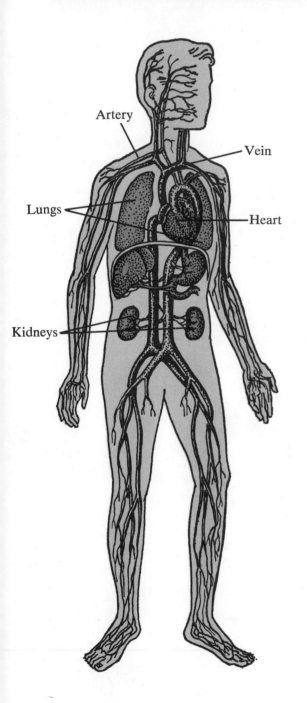

Artery

Vein

Lungs

Heart

Kidneys

How does blood travel around your body?

Your blood makes a round trip through your body in less than a minute, thousands of times a day. It travels through tubes called blood vessels. There are three main kinds of blood vessels—arteries (ARE-tuh-reez), veins (VANES), and capillaries (CAP-ih-ler-eez).

When blood is pumped out of your heart it goes into your largest arteries. These branch into smaller arteries, which branch into still smaller ones. The blood flows from the smallest arteries into your capillaries.

Capillaries are bridges between your arteries and your veins. They are the tiniest blood vessels, so small that you cannot see them without a microscope. Blood travels from the capillaries into tiny veins. These lead to larger and still larger veins. Finally, the largest veins take the blood back to your heart.

Why do you need blood?

Blood feeds your cells, cleans them, and works to keep them healthy. It carries food and oxygen to every cell of your body. The food and oxygen get into your cells by passing through the thin walls of your capillaries.

Blood cleans all your cells by picking up wastes from them. The wastes pass from your cells, through the capillary walls, into your blood. The wastes called urea (you-REE-uh) and uric acid are carried by the blood to your kidneys. There the wastes mix with water and then leave your body as urine (YOUR-in). The waste gas called carbon dioxide is carried by the blood to your lungs. It leaves your body when you breathe out.

Blood also protects you. It has special cells in it that fight germs.

How do your special blood cells fight germs?

The cells in your blood that fight germs are called "white cells." These are like an army for your body. They kill harmful germs that get into your blood. When a large number of germs enter your body, the number of white-cell "soldiers" grows. A lot of blood moves to the area where the germs are. The white-cell soldiers attack the germs and kill them. The used white cells and dead germs form the thick yellow liquid called pus. If the pus is inside a sore on your skin, it may leak out.

Why do you bleed?

A cut bleeds because it has opened some of your arteries, veins, or capillaries. Most cuts don't cause much bleeding because they open only the very small blood vessels. Because these vessels are narrow, blood moves through them very slowly, and comes out of them very slowly, too. If you should ever cut a large vein or artery, you would bleed very heavily.

Why do people stop bleeding?

Most people are born with a natural protection against losing too much blood. As soon as a cut starts to bleed, your body goes to work to stop it. The blood clots—thickens—and stops flowing. Soon you will see a scab on the cut. The scab is nothing more than dried, clotted blood.

If you are bleeding heavily, you can help blood clot faster by pressing on the cut or by bandaging it. But that isn't necessary with a small cut. It will clot all by itself.

What are black-and-blue marks?

Black-and-blue marks are signs of bleeding under your skin. When you cut yourself you break open blood vessels and you bleed. When you bump into something, you may also break open blood vessels. But since your skin isn't broken, the blood can't come out. It stays under your skin, where its red coloring changes to yellow, green, and blue. When these colors show through your skin, we say you have a black-and-blue mark.

How much blood do you have in your body?

If you weigh about 100 pounds, you have about seven pounds of blood in your body. That much blood would fill about four quart-size milk containers. If you weigh less, you have less blood. When you become an adult, you will probably have enough blood to fill five or six quart-size milk containers.

Why is blood red?

Blood looks as if it's solid red, but it's not. If you look at blood under a microscope, you will see that it is made up of several different kinds of cells. Only one kind is red. But this one kind gives blood its red color.

 Your blood has about 18 billion (18,000,000,000) red cells in it!

What makes your foot "go to sleep"?

Sometimes, after you have been sitting on your foot, you get a prickly feeling in it. That feeling means that not enough blood has been moving through your foot. You have been squeezing the veins and arteries so that blood could barely pass through them. When this happens, your blood can't carry the wastes out of your cells. Your nerve cells become "poisoned" with wastes. They aren't able to send messages to your brain. Your foot feels numb, and we say it has "gone to sleep." But when you get up and stretch your foot out again, blood suddenly starts flowing again. The nerves in your foot begin to send a lot of messages to your brain. You feel all the activity as "pins and needles" pricking your foot.

Keeping Healthy

What are drugs?

Drugs are anything you take into your body, besides food, that makes your body change. If the change mainly helps your body, the drug is called a medicine. If the change mainly harms your body, the drug is called either a poison or a narcotic (nar-KOT-ick). A poison will make you very sick or will kill you. A narcotic is a habit-forming drug. Once you have a lot of it in your body, you need to keep taking it all the time. Otherwise you may feel nervous, get terrible body aches, or have other problems. Doctors sometimes give small doses of narcotics such as codeine (KOE-deen) or morphine (MORE-feen) to patients as medicines. These narcotics are helpful because they can stop pain.

Other drugs that doctors consider helpful are aspirin and penicillin. Some drugs that doctors consider harmful are heroin (HEHR-o-in), a very dangerous narcotic that is illegal for anyone to use, and nicotine (NICK-uh-teen), a poison found in cigarettes.

Almost all drugs—medicines or not—have a very powerful effect on the body. If too much of any drug gets into your body, it can make you sick or kill you. It is against the law to take most drugs without a doctor's permission.

What are germs?

Germs are tiny living things, so small that you cannot see them without a microscope. Some are called bacteria (back-TEER-ee-uh), and some are called viruses. They are everywhere around us and in us. Viruses and some bacteria

are harmful. If they get into your body, they grow very rapidly. Harmful germs can give you a cough, a fever, or the measles.

You can help protect yourself from harmful germs by keeping your body clean and strong—and by being careful who you share your straws with!

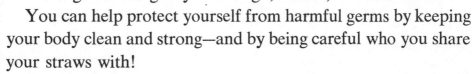

What is a virus?

A virus is a kind of germ that can cause you to get sick. Many viruses are so small that you can't see them through an ordinary microscope. You must have a very powerful instrument, an electron microscope, to see them. Doctors often know that viruses are in your body even if they can't see them. Special signs, called symptoms, appear in your body when it is fighting viruses. The lumpy, swollen neck you get with mumps and the high fever you get with flu are all symptoms. Doctors can often tell from symptoms just which viruses are at work in your body. And they can give you medicines to help you feel better.

Why can't you get the chicken pox more than once?

When you get sick, your white blood cells begin fighting the harmful germs in your body. One of the ways that the white cells fight is by making special germ-killers called antibodies. White cells make antibodies for each particular sickness.

If you get the chicken pox, your white cells make chicken pox antibodies. After you are better, these antibodies stay in your blood and keep killing any chicken pox viruses that get into your body. That is why you can't get chicken pox twice. You have become "immune" to the chicken pox.

What do shots do for you?

Some shots let your body make antibodies for a disease, without your ever having to get that disease. When your doctor gives you a shot for whooping cough, he puts a special liquid into your body. It causes your body to make antibodies against whooping cough germs. Then you become immune to whooping cough.

Sometimes your doctor gives you a shot of a "serum." Serum already has antibodies in it. It takes the place of your own antibodies and protects you against a particular disease.

If harmful bacteria have made you sick, your doctor may give you a shot of medicine. The medicine kills bacteria faster and better than your own white cells and antibodies can. Then you get well more quickly. So far scientists have not discovered any medicine that can kill viruses.

Will you catch cold if you get caught in the rain on a chilly day?

Probably not. You cannot catch a cold simply by getting caught in the rain. Viruses must start to grow inside your nose or throat before you can get a cold. Scientists believe that these viruses get into your body when you breathe. When someone with a cold coughs or sneezes, many virsuses escape into the air. If you are nearby, you can breathe in these viruses. If your body doesn't fight them off before they grow, you get the cold.

A chill from the rain may make your body weaker than it normally is. If some viruses are already in your nose or throat, your body won't be able to keep fighting them off. Or if you breathe in some viruses while you are chilled, your body may be too weak to kill them right away. Then they will grow and spread, and you will get a cold.

Why can you get many colds?

When you get a cold, your body makes antibodies to fight the particular virus that has come into your body. You will never get a cold from that kind of virus again. However, more than 200 different kinds of viruses can cause colds. So, if a new cold virus enters your body, you will not have antibodies in your blood to fight it. Then you will get another cold.

47

What are tonsils?

Tonsils are found all the way in the back of your mouth, at the top of your throat. You have one tonsil on each side of your throat. Tonsils trap harmful germs that come in through your mouth, and they make extra white blood cells to fight these germs.

When you get a sore throat, your tonsils will often swell up. They swell because they are working to help your throat get well, not because anything is wrong with them.

Until recently, doctors used to remove the tonsils from children who often had swollen tonsils and sore throats. They thought that the swollen tonsils were causing the sore throats. But now they know that the sore throats are causing the swollen tonsils. So they treat the sore throats, and they don't remove the tonsils.

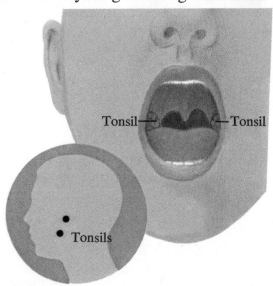

Tonsil— —Tonsil

Tonsils

What is fever?

Fever is a body temperature that is a lot higher than normal. It is usually a sign that you have germs growing somewhere inside you.

Your body is always making heat. Normally, a special part of your brain controls your temperature, keeping it at 98.6°F. When you feel cold, this part of your brain sends messages to certain muscles to make you shiver. When you feel hot, it sends messages to your skin to make you sweat. But when you get sick, the germs in your body upset this special part of your brain, and your temperature goes up. Certain medicines can bring the temperature back to the right level again.

Did You Know That...

Everyone has fat in his or her body. There is a layer of fat right under your skin. It helps to protect your bones from bumps. The layer of fat keeps your body warm when the weather is cold, and cool when the weather is hot. If you were on a desert island with no food, your body could use this fat as an emergency food supply. A little fat can help your body, but too much fat means it's time to go on a diet.

If you counted the hairs on your head, they would probably add up to more than 100,000.

Water makes up a big part of your body weight—about three-fifths of it. Even your bones are made up of about one-quarter water.

The hardest part of your body isn't your head. It's the enamel that coats your teeth.

As you grow older, you need less sleep. A newborn baby spends more time asleep than awake. Most adults need about eight hours of sleep a day.

In one day of breathing, more than 10,000 quarts (11,000 liters) of air go in and out of your lungs. That's enough to blow up about 675 beach balls.

NOT HAVING A STATION WAGON PRESENTS SOMETHING OF A PROBLEM.

If you have an average appetite, you'll probably eat more than 35 tons of food in your lifetime. You would need 70 station wagons to bring home such a large grocery order.

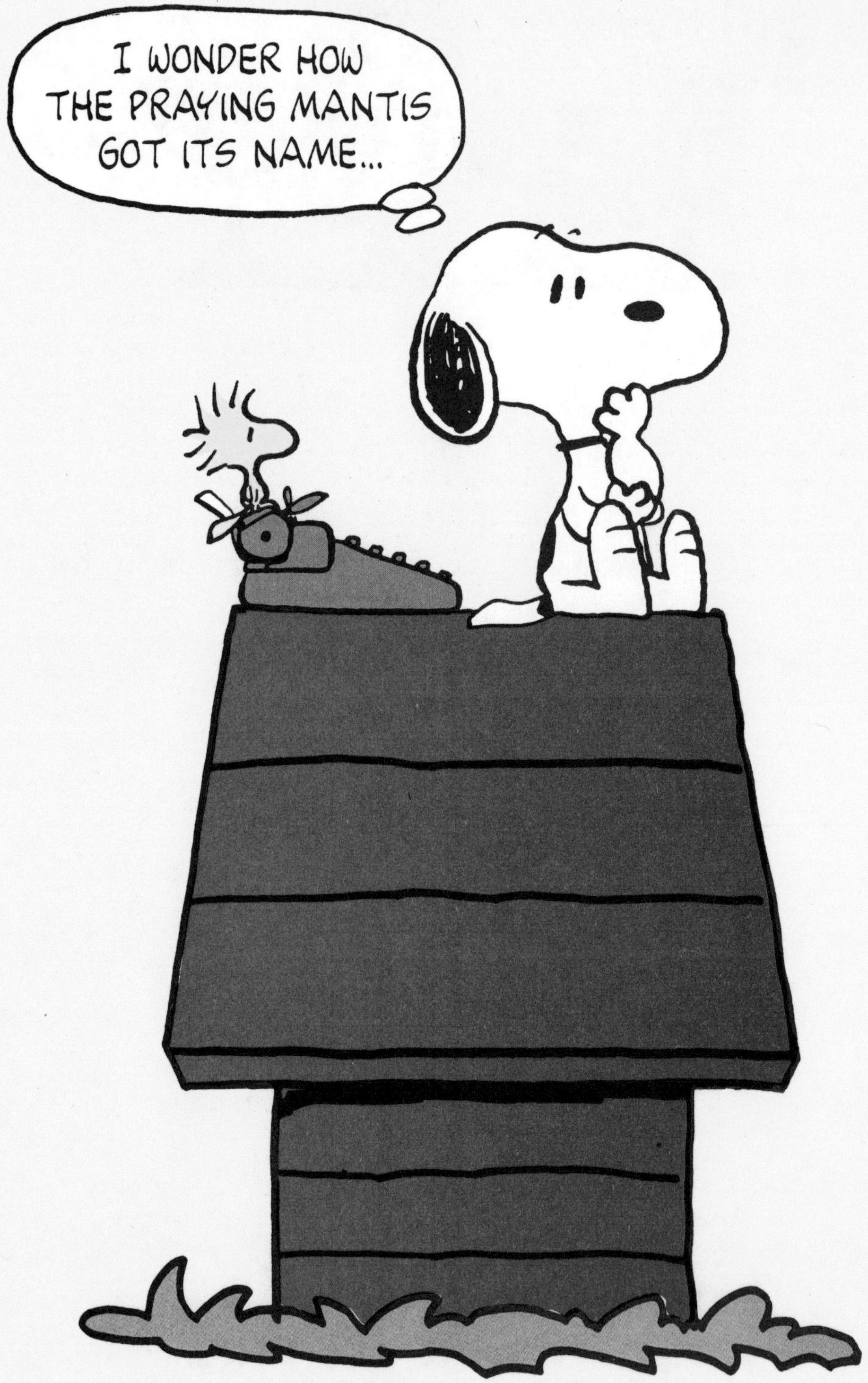
I WONDER HOW THE PRAYING MANTIS GOT ITS NAME...